Dear Parent:

Do you want to spark your child's creativity? Do you want your child to become a confident writer? Road to Writing can help.

Road to Writing is a unique creative writing program that gives even the youngest writers a chance to express themselves. Featuring five distinct levels, or Miles, the Road to Writing program accompanies children from their first attempts at writing to comfortably writing on their own.

A Creative Start
For children who "write" stories by drawing pictures
• easy picture prompts • familiar subjects • places to draw

Creative Writing With Help
For children who write easy words with help
• detailed picture prompts • places to draw and label

Creative Writing On Your Own
For children who write simple sentences on their own
• basic story starters • popular topics • places to write

First Journals
For children who are comfortable writing short paragraphs
• more complex story starters • space for free writing

Journals
For children who want to try different kinds of writing
• cues for poems, jokes, stories • brainstorming pages

There's no need to hurry through the Miles. Road to Writing is designed without age or grade levels. Children can progress at their own speed, developing confidence and pride in their writing ability along the way.

Road to Writing—"write" from the start!

Look for these
Road to Writing
books

Mile 1

Mile 2

Mile 3

Tips for Using this Book

- Help your child read each page. Then let your child draw or write a response—right in the book!

- Don't worry—there are no "right" or "wrong" answers. This book is a place for your child to be creative.

- Remind your child to write at his or her own pace. There's no rush!

- Encourage your child with plenty of praise.

Pencils, pens, and crayons are all suitable for use in this book. Markers are not recommended.

A GOLDEN BOOK • New York
Golden Books Publishing Company, Inc. New York, New York 10106

ISBN: 0-307-45405-3

A MM

GET A CLUE!

by Mel Friedman, Ellen Weiss, and

_____

(your name)

illustrated by
Rick Stromoski and

_____

(your name)

You just opened your own detective agency.

Write your name on the sign.

Draw a picture of yourself
in your detective clothes.

You are at the detective store
to buy some tools.

What are you going to buy?

Pick some, or make up your own.

_____magnifying glass

_____compass

_____notebook

_____tape recorder

_____

_____

Draw your tools in your detective case.

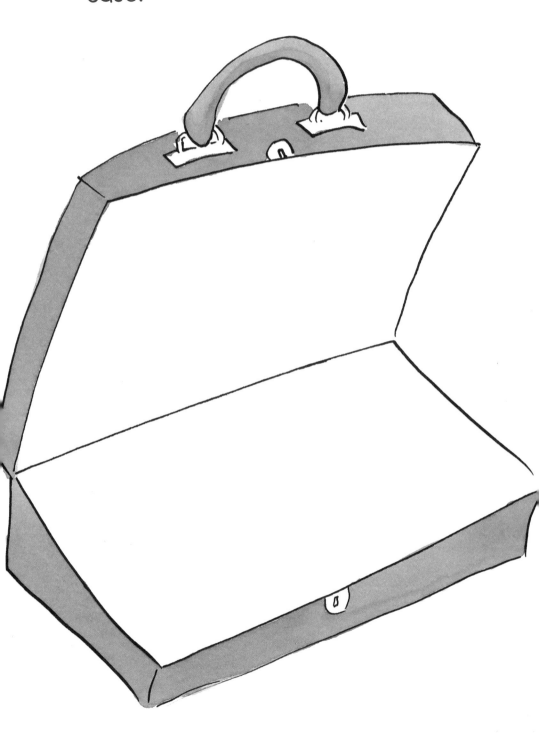

Kid Detective Magazine just arrived in the mail.

Draw the picture on the cover.

KID DETECTIVE
M A G A Z I N E **FREE**

NEW DISGUISES
FOR SPRING

DECODER RINGS:
DO THEY REALLY
WORK?

Join the *Kid Detective Magazine* club.

Fill out the form.

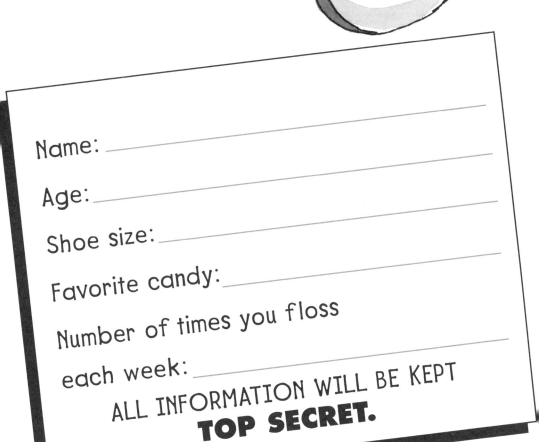

Name: _____

Age: _____

Shoe size: _____

Favorite candy: _____

Number of times you floss each week: _____

ALL INFORMATION WILL BE KEPT **TOP SECRET.**

It's your first case!
A note was slipped under your door.
Fill in the note.

Dear _____ ,

(your name)

I have a problem, and I need

your help!

Meet me at two o'clock at the

_____ .

(a place)

Come alone!

Draw a picture of the meeting place.

The note was from a girl who lost her dog. Help her find him.

Write down the clues in your detective notebook.

Name of dog:

_____

Color of dog:

_____

Dog's favorite snack:

_____

Dog was last seen at:

_____

Draw a picture of the missing dog.

You found a trail of paw prints.
Where do they lead?

List some places.

#1. library

#2. school

#3. bank

Where else?

#4. _____

#5. _____

#6. _____

Use the words in the list to
fill in the blanks.

Pass the _____ on the right.
(place #2)

Turn left at the _____.
(place #6)

Go around the _____.
(place #3)

Turn right at the _____.
(place #5)

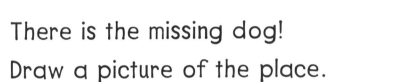

There is the missing dog!
Draw a picture of the place.

There's a story in the newspaper about you.

Finish the story.

Super Detective!

Today, Detective _____
(your name)

found a lost dog. The dog was found

at the _____.
(place where dog was found)

The dog's owner is _____
(a feeling)

to have the dog back.

Draw the picture that appears in the paper.

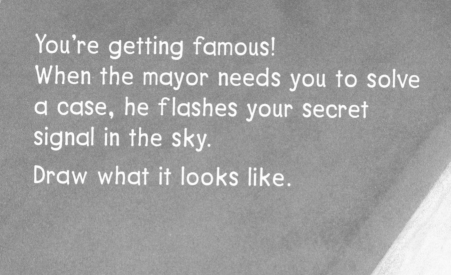

You're getting famous!
When the mayor needs you to solve
a case, he flashes your secret
signal in the sky.

Draw what it looks like.

The mayor has given you a secret
name, too.

It is _____.

How do you get around town?
Pick one, or make up your own.

by bicycle

by donkey

by helicopter

by_____

Draw a picture of yourself on the way to a case.

You are following a clue down a
dark alley.
Pick a word to write on the sign,
or make up your own.
Then finish the picture.

SHARKS   FROGS
PORCUPINES   MICE

You have another case.
Mrs. Rich is missing a pie!
Write down the clues.

What kind of pie is it?

_____

What time did the pie disappear?

_____ o'clock

Who is the pie for?

_____

Draw a sketch of
the missing pie.

There were five people in Mrs. Rich's kitchen when the pie disappeared. Could one of them be the thief?

Write down the people who were in the kitchen.

the baker

the mailman

Who else?

_____

_____

_____

Draw pictures of these people.

This case is harder than you thought. (None of those people took the pie.)
You ask Mrs. Rich more questions.

She says the pie was in the window.

Then there was a huge wind.

Draw what you think happened next.

Mrs. Rich gives you a reward
for solving the case.
It's a ticket for a trip!

"Where are
you going?"

"I'm going to
_____!"

Draw a picture of yourself
on the trip.

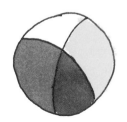

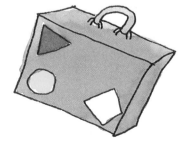

Your detective business is growing. You need to hire a partner.

Describe your perfect partner.

WANTED: PARTNER

Should be:

clever

_____

_____

_____

_____

_____

_____

Draw a picture of your perfect partner.

What's your favorite disguise?
Pick one, or make up your own.

a funny hat

a mustache

a long wig

a raincoat

a _____

Draw pictures of you and your partner in disguise.

It's your toughest case yet.
Somebody stole second base!

Your partner filled in some of these
clues. Fill in the rest.

The name of the home team:

The Mighty Monkeys

The name of the visiting team:

The last person who was near second base:

The second baseman
_____

The person who discovered the base was missing:
_____

Draw a sketch of the baseball field.

It turns out the base wasn't stolen after all!
What happened was...
(Pick one.)

_____Player #5 took it by mistake.

_____A dog thought it was a bone and buried it.

_____The coach's mom took it home to clean it.

Draw the base being taken.

You and your partner returned
the base to the home team.
Then they won the game!

Draw you and your partner
in the team photo.

The mayor has written you a note in code.

Decode it.

14 9 3 5

23 15 18 11!

A	B	C	D	E	F	G	H	I	J	K	L	M
1	2	3	4	5	6	7	8	9	10	11	12	13

Write a note back to the mayor in code.

N	O	P	Q	R	S	T	U	V	W	X	Y	Z
14	15	16	17	18	19	20	21	22	23	24	25	26

Someone (or something) left handprints on the wall.

Draw a picture of the person
(or thing) that left the prints.

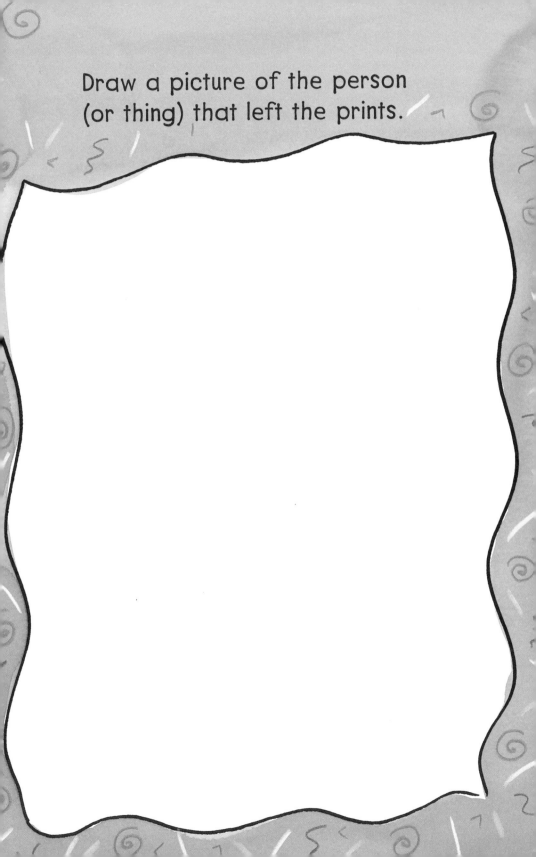

Hooray!
You've been named "Kid Detective of the Year" by *Kid Detective Magazine*.

Draw a picture of yourself on the cover.

KID DETECTIVE
M A G A Z I N E   FREE

NEW DETECTIVE
CRACKS CASE

THIS KID IS
GOOD!
REAL GOOD!